Mythical Creatures

GIANTS

Martha London

DiscoverRoo
An Imprint of Pop!
popbooksonline.com

abdobooks.com

Published by Pop!, a division of ABDO, PO Box 398166, Minneapolis, Minnesota 55439.

Printed in the United States of America, North Mankato, Minnesota.

102019
012020

THIS BOOK CONTAINS RECYCLED MATERIALS

Cover Photo: Shutterstock Images
Interior Photos: Shutterstock Images, 1, 6, 7, 10–11 (bottom), 13 (bottom), 14 (top), 15 (bottom), 17, 19, 20–21, 23, 26–27, 28, 31; C. E. Brock/Album/British Library/Alamy, 5; Chronicle/Alamy, 8, 9; iStockphoto, 10 (map), 12–13 (top), 14 (bottom), 18, 24, 25; Pictorial Press Ltd/Alamy, 15 (top), 30; Art Collection 2/Alamy, 29

Editor: Sophie Geister-Jones
Series Designer: Jake Nordby

Library of Congress Control Number: 2019942460

Publisher's Cataloging-in-Publication Data

Names: London, Martha, author.

Title: Giants / by Martha London

Description: Minneapolis, Minnesota : Pop!, 2020 | Series: Mythical creatures | Includes online resources and index.

Identifiers: ISBN 9781532165771 (lib. bdg.) | ISBN 9781532167096 (ebook)

Subjects: LCSH: Mythical animals--Juvenile literature. | Giants--Juvenile literature. | Folklore--Juvenile literature. | Legends--Juvenile literature. | Animals and history--Juvenile literature.

Classification: DDC 398.45--dc23

WELCOME TO DiscoverRoo!

Pop open this book and you'll find QR codes loaded with information, so you can learn even more!

Scan this code* and others like it while you read, or visit the website below to make this book pop!

popbooksonline.com/giants

*Scanning QR codes requires a web-enabled smart device with a QR code reader app and a camera.

TABLE OF CONTENTS

CHAPTER 1

GUARDING THE FOREST

One evening, a man got lost in a mountain forest. As it got dark, he began to light a fire. The fire sparked and the man noticed a giant sleeping nearby. He had bushy red hair. The giant woke up.

WATCH A VIDEO HERE!

Kind giants are rare in European stories.

"What are you doing in my forest?" the giant demanded.

“I’m sorry,” the man said. “I didn’t mean to bother you. I’m just trying to get back to my village.”

The giant was pleased with the man’s polite answer. “I’ll help you,” he replied.

In Thai legends, a Yak is a guardian giant.

Using his huge hand, the giant picked the man up. Then he carried the man home in three big steps.

DID YOU KNOW? **In some stories, a giant can cross a mountain in one step.**

CHAPTER 2

GIANTS IN HISTORY

Legends about giants exist all around the world. Some of the most famous stories come from ancient Greece and northern Europe.

LEARN MORE HERE!

In Jack and the Beanstalk, *Jack climbs up a beanstalk to steal from a giant's home.*

PLACES WITH MYTHS ABOUT GIANTS

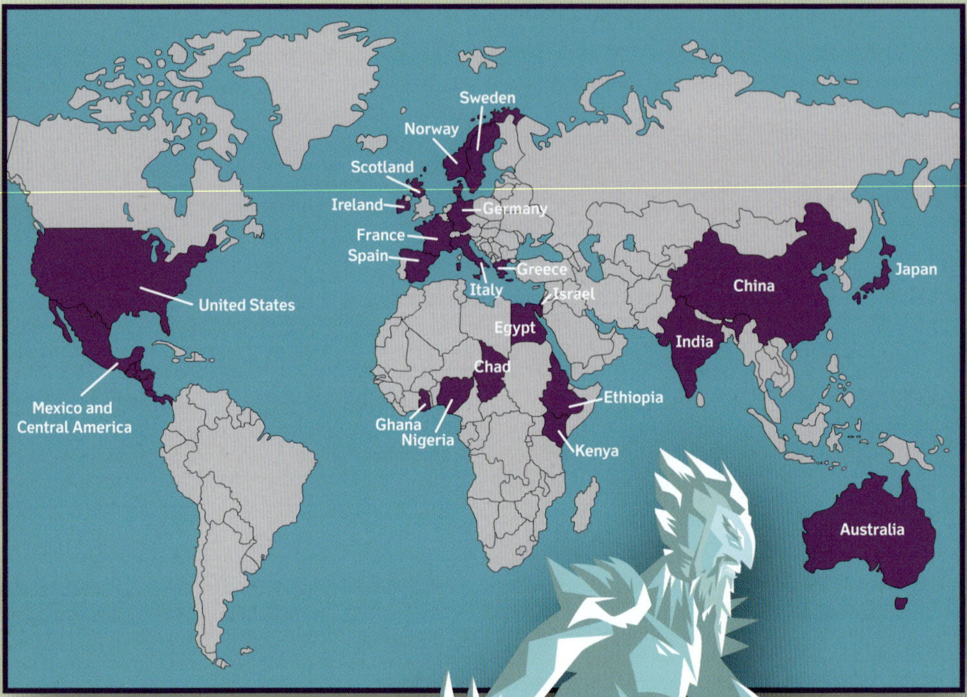

In **Norse** myths, giants are very powerful. They are related to the gods. In one myth, the Norse god Thor fights a giant. His hammer shatters the giant's stone club. Thor defeats the giant.

DID YOU KNOW?

In Japan, people use soybeans to keep giants away.

Thor defeated a giant named Hrungnir.

Greek myths tell stories of powerful giants too. There was a war between gods and giants. The gods won. To

Many mountain ranges are named after sleeping giants. Some people believed the sun turned giants to stone.

punish the giants, the gods locked them under mountains.

GIANTS THROUGH THE YEARS

700S BCE

The ancient Greeks write myths about giants.

900 CE

Norse legends tell the story of the gods punishing giants.

200 BCE

A Maya legend tells of a giant causing earthquakes.

2016
The BFG is a movie about a friendly giant.

1750
A German writer collects stories about a giant named Rubezahl who guards the mountains.

1963
A Book of Giants collects fairy tales about giants from several countries in Europe.

CHAPTER 3

MORE THAN GIANT

In most myths, giants look like large humans. Giants have long hair on their heads. Male giants usually have beards. But there are many different descriptions of giants.

COMPLETE AN ACTIVITY HERE!

Some stories say giants have magic powers. But many stories just say giants are strong and large.

A giant's size also depends on the story. British myths say giants are 12 feet (3.5 m) tall. Other myths tell of giants that are 40 feet (12 m) tall.

DID YOU KNOW?

A Japanese giant called an *oni* has red or blue skin and horns on its head.

In some stories, giants were so tall they could reach the clouds.

Cyclops were good at making objects out of metal, such as swords.

Other myths describe giants with only one eye. In Greek myths, these giants are called **cyclops**. They herded sheep. One-eyed giants exist in many other **cultures** too. For example, Balor is a one-eyed giant from Ireland.

CHAPTER 4

GIANT ATTITUDE

Giants' large size makes them very strong. They can easily lift huge objects. And they are good at fighting. In many **legends**, giants are dangerous. They destroy villages and try to trick people.

LEARN MORE HERE!

People once believed that ancient sites such as Stonehenge were built by giants.

Paul Bunyan is a giant that lived in North America and worked as a lumberjack.

Most stories say giants lived in dark forests and far-away mountains. People stayed away from these places. They were afraid of being hurt or killed.

DID YOU KNOW?

In one story, giants lifted huge sections of land. They threw the land into the ocean to create islands.

Many myths say giants are stupid. Myths say people can **outsmart** giants. It is not possible to beat a giant using strength alone. People must use their brains to trick a giant.

Most giants smell bad because they do not wash themselves.

But not all giants are mean. Some giants attack only if people **offend** them. These giants are kind to nice people. Most giants want to be left

Atlas is a Greek giant that is in charge of holding up Earth.

The giant Kumbhakarna ate the god Hanuman's monkey army.

alone. Some myths describe giants as being the first creatures on Earth. One **Norse** myth says the world was created from the body of a giant.

A GIANT APPETITE

Hindu legends told stories about a giant. The giant had a big **appetite**. He ate anything he could find. The gods cursed him. They made him sleep for six months of the year. But when the giant woke up, he was hungrier than ever. He ate everything in his path until he fell asleep again six months later. The cycle kept repeating.

MAKING CONNECTIONS

TEXT-TO-SELF

What would you do if you met a giant? Talk to a friend and compare your answers.

TEXT-TO-TEXT

Giants are part of many myths and legends. What myths or legends have you read about in other books?

TEXT-TO-WORLD

Why do you think so many cultures have stories about giants? Write a few sentences explaining your answer.

GLOSSARY

appetite – how hungry someone feels.

culture – the ideas, lifestyle, and traditions of a group of people.

cyclops – a type of giant with only one eye.

legend – a story passed down over many years.

Norse – relating to the countries of Norway, Sweden, Finland, and Denmark.

offend – to hurt a person's feelings.

outsmart – to defeat someone by thinking faster and tricking them.

INDEX

ONLINE RESOURCES

popbooksonline.com

Scan this code* and others like it while you read, or visit the website below to make this book pop!

popbooksonline.com/giants

*Scanning QR codes requires a web-enabled smart device with a QR code reader app and a camera.